R.M. Cottage

The writers of hymns ancient and modern

In their order of time and according to their churches

R.M. Cottage

The writers of hymns ancient and modern
In their order of time and according to their churches

ISBN/EAN: 9783742854568

Manufactured in Europe, USA, Canada, Australia, Japa

Cover: Foto ©ninafisch / pixelio.de

Manufactured and distributed by brebook publishing software
(www.brebook.com)

R.M. Cottage

The writers of hymns ancient and modern

THE

WRITERS

OF

𝕳𝖞𝖒𝖓𝖘 𝕬𝖓𝖈𝖎𝖊𝖓𝖙 𝖆𝖓𝖉 𝕸𝖔𝖉𝖊𝖗𝖓,

IN THEIR ORDER OF TIME AND ACCORDING TO THEIR CHURCHES,

WITH

NOTES

AND INDEX GIVING THE GREEK, LATIN AND GERMAN FIRST LINES.

R. M. COTTAGE,

N. VALENCE,

ALTON, HANTS.

Price Sixpence.

" I am a Member of the Church of England; I belong to the Ancient Historic Church of my Country; It is a living branch of the great universal Church of God; It is the Catholic Church of this land, which has ever held The Catholic Faith and Ritual; and protested against all false doctrine, heresy, and schism; It welcomes all who profess and call themselves Christians, and for eighteen centuries has taught the people of this nation to fear God, to regard man, and to follow our Saviour Christ. . . . It has ever sought the highest good of all classes in England, and whatever holy desires, good counsels and just works, our Kings, Lords and Commons have attained to have sprung from its holy teaching. It has produced patient sufferers, earnest labourers, wise reformers, and noble writers, whose deeds and words and verses have from age to age stirred the hearts and hands of all true Englishmen. . . . . In this Church I have lived; in this Church will I die."

DIARY OF SIR J. WINCHESTER.

Dedicated

TO

THE COMPILERS OF HYMNS ANCIENT AND MODERN,

THOSE CAREFUL GATHERERS FROM MANY SOURCES;

IN THE HOPE

THAT THE NEXT EDITION MAY STILL MORE WIDELY REPRESENT

THE VARIOUS AGES AND LANGUAGES AND PORTIONS OF

THE HOLY CATHOLIC AND APOSTOLIC CHURCH.

HYMN WRITERS

ANCIENT AND MODERN

𝔒𝔣 𝔱𝔥𝔢 ℭ𝔞𝔱𝔥𝔬𝔩𝔦𝔠 ℭ𝔥𝔲𝔯𝔠𝔥.

THE Hymn Writers are of every age and every branch of the Catholic Church. In Hymns Ancient and Modern we have Authors who belong to

The Church of Israel,
The Greek Church,
The Italian (or Roman) Church,
The English (or Anglican) Church,
The Irish Church,
The French (or Gallican) Church,
The Bohemian Church,
The German Church,
The Spanish Church,
The American Church,
The Indian Church,
And others,

> All Branches
> of the
> Catholic Church.

There is no Protestant Church; every Church protests against some error or evil.

There are also some Hymns written by persons who separated themselves from the Catholic Church of their country.

ANCIENT HYMN WRITERS.

MOSES, 1571—1451. Of the Jewish Church. Psalm 90, written towards the end of the wanderings on seeing his aged companions die—turned into Hymn 165 by Dr Watts.

DAVID, THE KING, 1055—1015. Of the Jewish Church.
Psalm 23, turned into H. 197 by Sir H. Baker.
Psalm 34, turned into H. 290 by Tate and Brady.
Psalm 42. When flying from Absalom. Turned into H. 238 by Tate and Brady.
Psalm 51, turned into H. 249.
Psalm 84. Written in exile. Turned into H. 237 by Lyte.
Psalm 98, turned into H. 378 by Sir H. Baker.
Psalm 100, turned into H. 166 by Hopkins or by Rev. W. Kethe.
Psalm 103, turned into H. 298 by Rev. F. H. Lyte.
Psalm 104, turned into H. 167 by Sir R. Grant.
Psalm 136, turned into H. 381 by Sir H. Baker.
Psalm 137, turned into H. 284 by Rev. F. H. Lyte.
Psalm 143, turned into H. 93 by J. Mardley.
Psalm 148, turned into H. 292 by J. Kempthorne.

SOLOMON, THE KING, 1015—975. Of the Jewish Church.
Psalm 72. Written when young, B.C. 1010. Turned into H. 219 by J. Montgomery; into H. 220 by Dr Watts.

A.D. In the year of our Lord.
4th Century—10th Century.

AMBROSE, ST., 340—397. Of the Italian Church. The great
Bishop of Milan[1].
H. 1, 2, 9, 10, 11, 12, 14, 15, 16, 47, 55, 85, 87, 113, 126,
128, 130, 144, 152, 163, 430, 442, 444, 455.
Some of these were probably written by imitators of the
Bishop and are called Ambrosian Hymns.

PRUDENTIUS, AURELIUS CLEMENS, 348—390. Of the Spanish
Church. H. 56, 68, 76. A Judge and Christian writer.
" The Horace of the Christians."

ANATOLIUS, ST., 458. Of the Greek Church. Patriarch of
Constantinople. H. 21, 285, 439.

FORTUNATUS VENANTIUS, 530—609. Of the French Church.
Bishop of Poictiers. H. 96, 97, 113, 147, 309, 449.

GREGORY, ST., 540—604. Of the Italian Church. The Great
Bishop of Rome[2]. H. 14, 85.

ANDREW, ST., 660—732. Of the Greek Church. Archbishop
of Crete. H. 91.

BEDE, THE VENERABLE, 671—735. Of the English Church.
A monk of Jarrow, on the Tyne. A translator of the
Bible, and writer of English History. H. 415.

ST JOHN OF DAMASCUS, —780. Of the Greek Church. A
Priest of Jerusalem. H. 132, 133.

STEPHEN, ST., 725—794. Of the Greek Church. Of the
monastery of St Sabas, near the Dead Sea. H. 254.

COSMAS, ST., 700—760. Of the Greek Church. Bishop in the
Holy Land. Foster-brother of St John Damascene. H.
60.

CHARLEMAGNE, 742—814. Of the French Church. Emperor
of France and Germany. H. 157, 347.

THEODULPHUS, ST., 821. Of the French Church, made Bishop
of Orleans by Charlemagne. H. 98, written in prison.

JOSEPH, ST., 830. Of the Greek Church. A Monk of the
Studium, a monastery in Constantinople. H. 224, 423,
441.

GODESCALCUS, 950. Of the Swiss Church. A Monk of St
Gall. H. 295.

---

[1] The friend of St Augustine of Africa. Writer of the *Te Deum?*
The Rebuker of the Emperor; Teacher of Antiphonal Singing. Stern,
austere, and courageous.

[2] Sender of Augustin to England. Writer of many Collects in our
Prayer Book. Composer of the Gregorian Tones.

10th Century—14th Century.

ROBERT[1], THE KING, 970—1031. Of the French Church. King of France. H. 156.

FULBERT, ST., 1020. Of the French Church. Bishop of Chartres. H. 125.

BERNARD, of Morlaix in Brittany, 1150. Of the French Church. Of English birth. A Monk of Clugny. H. 225, 226, 227, 228[2].

BERNARD, ST., 1091—1153. Of the French Church. The Great Abbot of Clairvaux in Champagne[3]. H. 111, 177, 178, 189, 190.

ADAM OF ST VICTOR, 1100. Of the French Church. A Monk of the St Victor Monastery. H. 64, 82, 434.

AQUINAS, ST THOMAS[4], 1227—1274. Of the Italian Church. A Dominican Friar. H. 309, 310, 311, 312.

THOMAS OF CELANO[5], 1255. Of the Italian Church. A Franciscan Monk. H. 206, 398.

BONAVENTURA[6], ST., 1221—1274. Of the Italian Church. A Cardinal. H. 105.

JACOPONUS OR JAMES DE BENEDICTIS[7], 1306. Of the Italian Church. A Franciscan Monk. H. 117.

ANGLO-SAXON Hymn Book. H. 158.

PRAYER-BOOKS.

In the Middle Ages our forefathers had small Prayer Books which they called Breviaries. Amongst these Prayers

[1] "The gentlest of men." A great musician. A greatly afflicted king, and friend of St Fulbert.

[2] A poem of 3000 lines on the "evil world." As a contrast he describes the glory of Heaven.

[3] "The best monk that ever lived." Queller of heresies, Umpire between Kings, Counsellor of Popes, Founder of the Carthusian Order, Author of a Crusade. The Last of the Fathers. Foremost of the Middle Age Poets. Full of Scripture.

[4] "The Angelic Doctor." A great scholar. Founder of the Thomists against the Scotists.

[5] A friend of St Francis of Assisi.

[6] The Seraphic Doctor. Gave the Bible to the poor.

[7] A "memorable man," much persecuted. He became "a fool for Christ's sake."

were often Hymns, just as in our Common Prayer-Book we have the Hymn "Come Holy Ghost, our souls inspire," and many of Tate and Brady's Psalms and Hymns.

In England there were the Sarum, the York, the Hereford Breviaries or Prayer Books.

In France there were the Paris, the Le Mans, the Cluniac, the Meaux Prayer-books.

In Italy, the Roman Prayer Book.

In Germany, the Stuttgard, the Magdeburg.

In Spain, the Mozarabic.

In Belgium, the Liege Prayer Books.

The Authors of the Hymns are often not known.

SARUM or SALISBURY Prayer Book (Breviary). H. 45, 46, 57, 63, 88, 89, 95, 128, 141, 214, 396.

HEREFORD Prayer Book (Breviary). H. 56.

PARIS Prayer Book (Breviary). The Hymns in this were mainly composed in the 18th century by the two Santeuils and by C. Coffin. H. 13, 33, 41, 42, 43, 44, 48, 50, 54, 58, 65, 70, 71, 77, 78, 83, 84, 103, 146, 175, 208, 262, 273, 395, 405, 407, 429, 431, 432, 433, 443, 447, 451, 458.

LE MANS Prayer Book (Breviary). H. 34.

CLUNIAC Prayer Book (Breviary). H. 66.

MEAUX Prayer Book (Breviary). H. 72.

ROMAN Prayer Book (Breviary). H. 15, 16, 38, 45, 85, 100, 101, 102, 127, 129, 180, 232, 347, 396, 452, 457, 459.

STUTTGARD Prayer Book (Breviary). H. 86, 295.

MAGDEBURG Prayer Book (Breviary). H. 82.

MOZARABIC Prayer Book (Breviary). H. 104, 296.

LIEGE Prayer Book (Breviary). H. 179.

OFFICE BOOKS FOR HOLY COMMUNION.

In the Middle Ages our ancestors had books for the Office of the Holy Communion which they called Missals. In these were Hymns, as in the Communion Office of our Common Prayer Book we have the "Ter Sanctus" Hymn, "Holy, Holy, Holy, Lord God of hosts," and the "Gloria in Excelsis" Hymn, "Glory be to God on high." In England there was the Sarum or Salisbury Missal or Office for Holy Communion. In France, the Paris Holy Communion Office (Missal). In Italy, the Roman. In Germany, the Mentz and others.

16th and 17th Centuries.

PARIS Holy Communion Office (Missal). H. 49, 83, 117, 131, 156, 398.
ROMAN Holy Communion Office (Missal). H. 98.
MENTZ Holy Communion Office (Missal). H. 440.

The Church of Bohemia produced in the Middle Ages several Hymns in the Bohemian language. The Authors are not known. But in 1531 M. Weiss translated them into German. H. 136.

MODERN HYMN WRITERS.

WEISS, MICHAEL, —1540. Of the Church of Bohemia. A Pastor. Friend of Luther and Reformers. H. 136.
XAVIER, ST FRANCIS, 1506—1552. Of the Church of Spain. The great Missionary and Jesuit in India and Japan. H. 106.
MARDLEY, or MARCHANT, JOHN, 1562. Of the Church of England. H. 93.
STERNHOLD, THOMAS[1], 1549. Groom of the Robes to Henry VIII. "A most strict liver"—turned the Psalms into verse with
HOPKINS, JOHN, REV.[1], 1544. Church of England. H. 166?
KETHE, WM., REV.[1], 1555. Of the Church of England. Rector of Okeford, Dorset. An exile at Geneva, and Friend of John Knox. H. 166?
STEGMANN, 1588—1632. A Lutheran Bishop. H. 27.
RINGWALD, BARTHOLOMEW, 1530—1598. A Lutheran. H. 52.
COSIN, JOHN, RIGHT REV., 1594—1672. Church of England. Bishop of Durham[2]. H. 157.
RINCKART, MARTIN, 1586—1649. A Lutheran Pastor. H. 379.
BAKER, FRANCIS, 1565. A Romanist Priest. A Prisoner in the Tower under Queen Elizabeth. H. 236.
CROSSMAN, SAMUEL, REV., 1624—1683. Church of England. Canon of Bristol. A good man in an evil age. H. 233.

---

[1] "The piety of these three was better than their poetry, they drank more of Jordan than of Helicon."
[2] A true English Churchman misliked by Geneva and Rome.

10

17th Century.

Scheffler, John (Angelus), 1624—1677. A Lutheran. A physician. A Mystic. Left the Lutherans and joined the Church of Germany in 1653. H. 192.

De Santeuil, Claude, 1628—1684. Of the Gallican Church. Writer in Paris Breviary. H. 103.

De Santeuil, Jean Baptiste, 1630—1697. Of the French Church, Canon of St Victor, Paris. H. 65, 78, 273, 407, 422, 431, 432, 433, 443, 451.

Heinrich, Albert, 1604—1668. Of the German Church. Organist and Composer. H. 26.

Guiet, C., —1684. Gallican Churchman. H. 395.

De Geste, —1702. Gallican Churchman. Bishop of Saintes, France. H. 405.

Mason[1], John, Rev., —1694. Church of England. Rector of Water-Stratford, Bucks.

Ken[2], Thomas, 1637—1712. Of Anglican Church. The saintly Bishop of Bath and Wells. H. 3, 23.

Schütz, John Jacob, 1640—1690. A Lutheran. Lawyer; a Pietist. H. 292, 293.

Schmolcke, Benjamin, 1672—1737. A Lutheran Pastor. H. 389.

Rodigast, Samuel, 1649—1708. A Lutheran. Schoolmaster. A Pietist. H. 389.

Tate, Nahum, 1652—1715. Of Church of Ireland. Poet Laureate to King Wm. III.: Translator of Psalms with

Brady, Nicholas, Rev., 1659—1726. Church of England and Ireland. Rector of Stratford-on-Avon. H. 62, 237, 238, 249, 290.

Watts, Dr Isaac, 1674—1748. Independent Minister. Descended from a French Huguenot. H. 108, 165, 220, 299, 438.

Coffin, Charles, 1676—1749. Of the Gallican Church. A Jansenist or Evangelical. Writer in the Paris Pr. Bk. H. 33, 41, 42, 43, 44, 48, 58, 77, 83, 84, 146, 262.

Besnault, The Abbé, —1726. Of the Gallican Church. Priest of St Maurice at Sens, France. H. 70, 71.

Browne, Simon, Rev., 1680—1732. Independent Minister. H. 209.

[1] An imitator of George Herbert.
[2] Rebuker of Charles II. One of the seven Bishops sent to the Tower for fidelity to their Church, yet a nonjuror too loyal to James II. to do homage to William III.

11

17th to 19th Centuries.

SCHENK, THEODORE, —1727. A Lutheran Pastor. H. 427.

BYROM, JOHN, 1691—1763. Church of England. F. R. S. A Scientific Man. Teacher of Shorthand. H. 61.

DODDRIDGE, PHILIP, 1702—1751. Independent Minister at Northampton. His mother was of the Bohemian Church. H. 53, 268, 317.

WESLEY, JOHN, REV.[1], 1703—1791. Church of England. A Clergyman and Founder of the Order of Methodists. H. 319.

WESLEY[2], CHARLES, REV., 1708—1788. Church of England. The Poet. Of the Order of Methodists. H. 7, 8, 51, 60, 147, 193, 195, 202, 205, 221, 248, 270.

GELLERT, CHRISTIAN FEAR-GOD, 1715—1769. Lutheran Pastor. H. 140.

CENNICK, JOHN, 1717—1755. Church of England. Then Methodist and Moravian. H. 51.

WILLIAMS, WM., REV., 1717—1791. Church of England and Welsh Methodist. H. 196.

ZINZENDORF, COUNT, 1700—1760. Of the Moravian Church. Founder at Herrnhut of the Bohemian Hussites. An unworldly devoted Christian, Priest, Bishop, and Hymn Writer. H. 400.

GREGOR, CHRISTIAN, 1723—1801. Of Moravian Church. H. 400.

NEWTON[3], JOHN, REV., 1725—1807. Church of England. Rector of St Mary Woolnoth. H. 176.

SHIRLEY, WALTER, HON. AND REV., 1725—1786. Church of England. Rector of Loughrea, Galway. Friend of Lady Huntingdon. H. 109.

PERRONET, EDWARD, —1792. Church of England. Then Methodist, Huntingdonian and Independent. H. 300.

MADAN, MARTIN, REV., 1726—1790. Preacher at Lock Hospital. H. 60.

COWPER[4], WM., 1731—1800. Church of England. The Poet. H. 246, 260, 373, 374.

CLAUDIAS, MATTHIAS, 1743—1815. A Bank Manager at Hamburg. H. 383.

---

[1] "If they ever leave the Church of England," said he, "God will leave them."

[2] A Hymn writer of very deep and wide spiritual experience.

[3] Once sailor on a slave ship. A Founder of the Evangelical body.

[4] Author of the *Olney Hymns* and *John Gilpin*.

12

18th and 19th Centuries.

HAWEIS, THOS., REV., 1732—1820. Church of England. Rector of Aldwinkle. H. 283.

ALLEN, JAMES[1], 1734—1804. Church of E.. H. 109.

TOPLADY, A., REV., 1740—1778. Church of England. Rector of New Ottery, Devon. H. 184.

HILL, ROWLAND, REV., 1744—1833. English Church[2]. H. 435.

DUNCAN, MARY LUNDIE[3], 1814—1840. Church of Scotland. Wife of a Minister. H. 435.

BRUCE, MICHAEL, 1746—1767. Church of Scotland. Schoolmaster. H. 201.

MORRISON, JOHN, REV., 1749—1798. Church of Scotland. Minister in Caithness. H. 80.

CAMERON, WM., REV., 1751—1811. Church of Scotland. Minister of Kirk Newton. H. 438.

OSWALD, HENRY S., 1751—1837. A Lutheran. Privy-Councillor to King of Prussia. H. 286.

FLOWERDEW, MRS ALICE, 1759—1830. A Baptist. H. 388.

HUPTON, JOB, 1762—1849. A Lady Huntingdon's Preacher and Baptist. H. 302.

COOPER, E., REV., 1770—1833. Church of England. Rector of Yoxall, Staffordshire. Author of Sermons. H. 164.

KEMPTHORNE, J., REV., 1775—1838. Church of England. Rector of St Michael's, Gloucester, Son of Admiral K. H. 292 (?).

KELLY, THOS., REV., 1769—1855. Church of Ireland. Then a Dissenter. Son of a Judge. Friend of Burke and Romaine. H. 25, 139, 200, 301, 439.

SCOTT, WALTER, SIR, BART., 1771—1832. Church of Scotland. The Poet. H. 206.

AUBER, HARRIET, 1773—1862. Church of England. H. 207, 294.

MANT, RICHARD, RT REV., 1776—1848. Church of Ireland. Bishop of Down and Connor. Writer of Poems. H. 113, 161, 448.

CARLYLE, J., REV., 1758—1804. Church of England. Vicar of Newcastle-on-Tyne. H. 244.

[1] A true weathercock. Now an Inghamite, then Huntingdonian, then a Sandemanian, then quite Independent. Editor of the Kendal H. Book.
[2] The open air preacher. Founder of Surrey Chapel. A good earnest man, pious and humorous.
[3] Writer of "Jesus, tender Shepherd, hear me."

18th and 19th Centuries.

MARRIOTT, JOHN, REV., 1780—1825. Anglican Church. Rector of Church Lawford, Warwickshire. H. 163, 360.

COLLYER[1], W. BENGO, DR, 1782—1854. Independent Minister. A Popular Preacher. H. 52.

HEBER, REGINALD, RT REV., 1783—1826. Church of India. Bishop of Calcutta. H. 26, 160, 241, 358, 439.

WHITE, HENRY KIRKE, 1785—1806. Church of England. The Poet[2]. H. 291.

GRANT, ROBERT, SIR, BART., 1785—1838. Church of India. Governor of Bombay. Brother of Lord Glenelg. H. 167, 251.

CONDER, JOSIAH, 1789—1855. Independent. Editor of Eclectic Review. H. 318.

EDMESTON, JAMES, 1791—1867. Church of England. An Architect. H. 281.

MILMAN, DEAN, 1791—1868. Anglican Church. Dean of St Paul's. Poet and Historian. H. 99, 279, 399.

KEBLE, JOHN, REV., 1792—1866. Anglican Churchman. The saintly Vicar of Hursley. The Poet[3]. H. 4, 18, 24, 67, 143, 154, 168, 213, 261, 350.

LYTE, H. F., REV., 1793—1847. Church of England. Vicar of Brixham. H. 27, 218, 240, 245, 284, 298.

BATHURST, W. H., REV., 1796—. Church of England. Of Lydney Park, Gloucestershire. H. 272, 278.

MEINHOLD, 1797—1851. A Lutheran. H. 402.

OSLER, EDWARD, 1798—1863. Church of England. Naturalist and Surgeon. H. 320.

KNAPP, ALBERT, 1798—1864. An Evangelical Church Pastor. H. 325.

ARMSTRONG, JOHN, RT REV. Of the African Church. Bishop of Grahamstown. H. 353.

DOANE, G. W., RIGHT REV., 1799—1859. Of the American Church. Bishop of New Jersey. H. 199.

MONTGOMERY, JAMES, 1771—1854. Of the Moravian and English Church. The Poet. H. 110, 219, 231, 247, 297, 355, 445.

ELLIOTT, CHARLOTTE, 1789—1871. Church of England[4]. H. 255, 264, 269.

[1] So said Robert Hall, "Hate the Devil and Dr Collyer."
[2] Southey wrote his life.
[3] Author of *The Christian Year*, and Founder of the High Church Party.
[4] Sister of Henry Venn and Edward Elliott, and friend of Cæsar Malan.

19th Century.

HAVERGAL, FRANCES R., 1836—1879. Church of England. H. 186, 203, 212, 259, 307, 356.

CHURTON, E., REV., 1800—1874. Church of England. Archdeacon of Cleveland. H. 364.

SPITTA, CHARLES, 1801—1859. A Lutheran Pastor. His father was French, his mother a Jewess. H. 357.

BODEN, JAMES, REV., 1757—1841. Congregationalist Minister. H. 236.

ANSTICE, JOSEPH, 1808—1836. Church of England. Professor, King's College [1]. H. 276, 387.

GURNEY, J. H., REV., 1802—1862. Church of England. Rector of St Mary's, Marylebone. H. 174, 267, 339, 375.

BRIDGES, MATTHEW. Anglo-Catholic Church. Left it for Roman Catholic Church of Italy, 1848. H. 187, 304, 349.

WILLIAMS, ISAAC, REV., 1802—1865. Church of England. The Poet of Stinchcombe. H. 33, 40, 65, 94, 262, 282, 395, 414, 429, 431, 433, 443, 451.

CHANDLER, JOHN, REV., 1805—1867. Anglican Church. Vicar of Whitley. Translator of Latin H. H. 2, 13, 38, 39, 41, 42, 43, 44, 48, 50, 71, 77, 78, 83, 84, 103, 146, 150, 151, 175, 208, 239, 273, 336.

CHAMBERS, JOHN D., 1803. Church of E. Recorder of Salisbury. H. 158.

ADAMS, SARAH F., 1805—1849. Church of E. Then Unitarian. H. 277.

OAKELEY, F., REV., —1882. Church of E. Left the Anglo-Catholic Church of E. for the Roman Catholic Church of Italy, 1845. H. 59, 105.

WHYTEHEAD, THOS., REV., 1815—1843. Church of New Zealand. Friend of Bp. Selwyn. H. 124.

HEATHCOTE, H. B., REV., 1812—1864. Church of England. Precentor of Salisbury. H. 29.

ALFORD, H., REV., 1810—1871. Anglican Churchman. Dean of Canterbury. Editor of the Greek Testament. H. 222, 328, 382, 392, 412, 462.

BODE, JOHN E., REV., 1816—1874. Church of England. Rector of Castle Camps, Cambridgeshire. Author of Ballads from Herodotus. H. 271.

FABER, F. W., REV., 1815—1863. Church of England. Left the Anglo-Catholic Church of his country for the Italian

---

[1] He wrote his Hymns when dying.

19th Century.

Church of Rome in 1846. H. 28, 114, 162, 169, 170, 223, 234, 324.

PUSEY, PHILIP, 1828—1879. Anglican Churchman. ? Son of Dr Pusey. H. 214.

CUMMINS, JAMES J., 1867. Church of England. H. 287.

NEALE, J. M., REV., 1818—1866. Church of England. Warden of Sackville College[1]. Original Hymns: 335, 352, 354, 385, 394. Jointly with J. Hupton: 302. Translations from Greek: H. 21, 91, 132, 133, 224, 254, 423, 441, 460. Translations from Latin: H. 1, 10, 11, 14, 15, 35, 45, 49, 56, 64, 75, 82, 85, 87, 88, 96, 97, 98, 104, 126, 128, 130, 144, 173, 177, 179, 225, 226, 227, 228, 232, 235, 295, 311, 313, 394, 396, 415, 430, 440, 442, 449, 455.

CAMPBELL, ROBERT, 1868. Left the Scottish Church for the Roman. A Lawyer at Edinburgh. H. 125, 127, 424, 434, 444.

LEESON, JANE E., 1864. H. 131, 334, 342.

SMYTTAN, GEORGE, REV., 1822—1855. Church of England. Rector of Hawksworth, Notts. H. 92.

WHITTEMORE, J. REV., 1802—1860. A Baptist. H. 342.

BAKER, HENRY, SIR, REV., BART.[2], 1821—1877. Church of E. Rector of Monkland, Gloucestershire. Original Hymns: 5, 89, 120, 171, 197, 211, 230, 242, 243, 250, 308, 323, 327, 344, 351, 363, 376, 378, 380, 381, 446, 450, 454, 468, 472. Jointly with Rev. W. Bullock: H. 242. Translations from Latin: H. 34, 57, 68, 100, 103, 111, 182, 432. Translation from German, H. 389.

BULLOCK, W., REV., 1798—1874. Church of Canada. Dean of Nova Scotia. H. 242, 377.

RORISON, G., REV., 1821—1869. Of the (Episcopal, the true) Church of Scotland. St Peter's, Peterhead. H. 163.

INGEMANN, BERNHARD S., 1789—1862. Of the Danish Ch. A Professor in Zealand. H. 274.

WHATELY, RICHARD, RIGHT REV., 1787—1863. Church of Ireland. Archbishop of Dublin. Friend of Dr Arnold. Opponent of the High Church Party. H. 26.

PALMER, WM., REV., 1810—1879. Left the Anglo-Catholic Church for the Roman Catholic in 1855. Elder brother of Earl Selborne. H. 422.

---

[1] Founder of East Grinstead Sisterhood. A learned, wise, and good High Churchman.

[2] One of the Compilers of *Hymns Ancient and Modern.*

19th Century.

Potter, Thos. J., Rev., 1827—1873. Roman Catholic Priest. H. 390.

Toke, Emma, Mrs, 1812—1878. Ch. of Ireland. Daughter of Dr Leslie, Bishop of Kilmore. H. 69, 149.

Collins, H., Rev., 1879. A Mission Priest with Father Lowder at the East End. Then, to his sorrow, he left Anglo-Catholic Ch. for Roman Catholic in 1860. Brother of the M.P. for Knaresborough.

Whiting, William, 1825—1878. Ch. of E. Master of Choristers' School, Winchester. H. 370.

Caswall, E., Rev., 1814—1877. From 1838—1847 a Deacon and Priest in English Ch.: then joined the Romish Ch., living and dying at Oratory, Edgbaston. H. 17, 47, 66, 76, 101, 102, 106, 107, 112, 117, 152, 156, 178, 180, 189, 253, 289, 303, 309, 311, 347, 407, 458, 459.

Cornish, Katharine D., Miss. H. 326.

Campbell, J. Montgomery, Miss, 1817—1878. Ch. of E. Translator of "O day most blest" from the French. H. 383.

Noel, Caroline M., Miss, 1820—1875. Ch. of E. Daughter of Hon. and Rev. Gerard Noel, Canon of Winchester. H. 336.

Winkworth, Catharine, Miss[1], 1820—1880. Ch. of E. Author of *Lyra Germanica.* H. 136, 192, 325, 379, 400, 402.

Chatfield, A. W., Rev., 1809—1881. Ch. of E. Vicar of Much Marcle, Herefordshire. H. 185, 461.

Sylvius. What is Sylvius? who is he? H. 457.

Irons, W. J., Rev., 1812—1883. Ch. of E. R. of St Mary Woolnoth, London. Son of a Dissenting Minister.

[1] The friend of Bunsen and a Translator of his Works.

LATER HYMN WRITERS.

ALEXANDER, C. F., MRS. Ch. of Ireland. Wife of Bishop of Derry. Author of "Hymns for Little Children" and Poems. H. 115, 119, 183, 229, 329, 331, 332, 403, 410, 411, 416, 418, 420.

ALDERSON, E. SIBBALD, MRS. Ch. of E. Sister of Dr Dykes, the composer. H. 121, 367.

BARING-GOULD, S., REV. Ch. of E. Rector of Lew Trenchard, Devon. Author of "Lives of the Saints." H. 274, 346, 391.

BENSON, R. M., REV. Ch. of E. One of the Cowley Fathers. H. 421, 452.

BICKERSTETH, E. H., REV. Ch. of E. Vicar of Christ Church, Hampstead. Author of a "Hymnal Companion" to Prayer-Book. H. 371.

BONAR, HORATIUS, DR. Scotch Free-Church Minister. H. 257, 258, 265, 288.

BORTHWICK, JANE, MISS. Ch. of Scotland. With Mrs Findlater her sister, author of "Hymns from Land of Luther," or H. L. L. H. 357.

BOURNE, W. ST HILL, REV. Ch. of E. Vicar of All Saints, Dalston. H. 333, 386.

BRIGHT, WM., REV., 1824. Ch. of E. Canon of Ch. Ch., Oxford. H. 6, 32, 181, 315, 322, 348, 404.

CLARK, J. H., REV. Ch. of E. Vicar of East Dereham, Norfolk. H. 447.

COLES, V. S. S., REV. Ch. of E. Rector of Shepton, Somerset. H. 321, 453, 456.

COMPILERS.

REV. F. H. MURRAY, R. of Chiselhurst.
    „   W. PULLING, R. of Eastnor.
    „   G. C. WHITE, V. of Newland,
         and others.

H. 1, 2, 10, 11, 13, 14, 15, 33, 35, 38, 39, 40, 41, 42, 43, 44, 45, 46, 47, 48, 49, 50, 54, 58, 59, 63, 64, 65, 66, 70, 71, 72, 75, 76, 77, 78, 80, 82, 83, 84, 85, 86, 87, 88, 90, 95, 96, 97, 101, 102, 104, 106, 108, 112, 117, 125, 126, 128, 129, 130, 135, 139, 141, 144, 146, 150, 151, 152, 156, 158,

173, 175, 177, 178, 179, 180, 200, 208, 232, 234, 235, 246, 289, 309, 310, 311, 314, 347, 395, 396, 405, 430, 433, 434, 440, 442, 443, 444, 449, 451, 455, 457, 458, 459.

COPELAND, W. J., REV. Ch. of E. Rector of Farnham, Essex. H. 63, 95, 141.

COX, FRANCES E., MISS. Ch. of E. Author of " Hymns from the German." H. 140, 286, 293, 427.

COXE, A. C., RT. REV. Ch. of America. Bishop of West New York. Author of " Christian Ballads." H. 359.

DANIELL, J. J., Rev. Ch. of E. Rector of Langley Burrell, Wilts. H. 341.

DIX, W. CHATTERTON. Ch. of E. A bookseller in Bristol. H. 79, 256, 316, 372, 384.

DOWNTON, H. Y., REV. Ch. of E. Vicar of Hopton, Suffolk. H. 73, 362.

ELLERTON, J., REV. Ch. of E. Rector of Barnes, Surrey. Editor of Ch. Hymns, and of " Notes on their Writers." Original: H. 30, 31, 37, 118, 397, 401, 406, 413, 419, 426. Translations : H. 12, 153, 296.

EVEREST, C. W., REV. Ch. of America. H. 263.

GURNEY, ARCHER J., REV. Ch. of E. Formerly Chaplain to the Court Church, Paris. H. 138.

HEWETT, J. W., REV., 1826. Ch. of E. Formerly Head Master of Bloxham School. Original: H. 216. Translations: H. 86, 90.

HORT, F. A. J., REV., 1829. Ch. of E. Hulsean Professor, Cambridge. Translations: H. 12, 153.

HENSLEY, LEWIS, REV., 1823. Ch. of E. Vicar of Hitchin, Herts. H. 217.

HOW, W. W., RIGHT REV. Ch. of E. Bishop of Bedford. Author of "Plain Words." H. 142, 198, 366, 417, 437.

HODGES, G. S., REV. Ch. of E. Vicar of Dunston, Stafford-shire. H. 340.

LITTLEDALE, R. F., REV. Ch. of E. Editor of " People's Hymnal." H. 466, 470.

MACLAGAN, W. D., RIGHT REV. Ch. of E. Bishop of Lichfield. H. 116, 122, 425, 428.

MAUDE, M. F., MRS. Ch. of E. Wife of the late Vicar of Chirk. H. 280.

MIDLANE, ALBERT, 1825. A Plymouth Brother. Writer of " Hymns for Children." H. 337.

MILLARD, J. E, REV., 1822. Ch. of E. Vicar of Basingstoke, Hants. H. 343

MILLER, EMILY H.   H. 300.
MORGAN, D. T.   Ch. of E.   H. 55, 145, 159.
MOULTRIE, GERARD, REV.   Vicar of Witney, Oxford.   Son of
    Dr Moultrie, the Poet of Rugby.   H. 408.
NEWMAN, J. H., REV., 1801.   An Anglo-Catholic till 1845,
    when he became a Roman Catholic; made Cardinal 1881.
    H. 9, 16, 172, 266.
PALMER, RAY, Dr, 1808.   American Congregational Minister.
    Kept his Golden Wedding Oct. 1882.   H. 190.
PLUMPTRE, E. H., REV.   Of Anglican Church.   Dean of Wells.
    Author of many Poems.   H. 345, 369, 393.
POLLOCK, J. B., REV.   Ch. of E.   Of St Albans, Birmingham.
    H. 471, 463, 464, 465, 469, 470.
POTT, F., REV.   Ch. of E.   Rector of Northill, Bedfordshire.
    H. 72, 135, 405.
PRYNNE, G. R., REV.   Ch. of E.   Vicar of St Peter's, Plymouth.
    H. 194.
ROBINSON, R. HAYES, REV.   Ch. of E.   Of St Michael's, Bath.
    H. 22.
SMITH, J. GREGORY, REV., 1830.   Anglican Ch.   Vicar of Gt
    Malvern. H. 123.
STONE, S. J., REV.   Ch. of E.   Vicar of St Paul's, Haggerstone.
    Author of "The Knight of Intercession," and "Lyra
    fidelium."   H. 215, 252, 361.
THRING, GODFREY, REV.   Of Anglo-Catholic Ch.   Rector of
    Alford, Somerset.   H. 19, 285, 305, 368.
TUTTIETT, L., REV.   Ch. of E.   Of Plumptre, Notts, and Scotch
    Episcopal Ch., St. Andrew's.   H. 74, 204.
TWELLS, H., REV.   Anglican Churchman, Rector of Waltham,
    Leicestershire.   H. 20.
WOODFORD, J. N., RIGHT REV.   Ch. of E.   Bishop of Ely.
    H. 58, 312.
WORDSWORTH, CHRISTOPHER, RT REV.   Of Eng. Ch.   Bishop
    of Lincoln.   Nephew of the Poet.   Author of "Hymns for
    Holy Days," "The Holy Year."   H. 275, 338, 365, 436.

INDEX TO ENGLISH FIRST LINES.

38. **Blest Creator.** Rev. J. CHANDLER, 1841, and Comps. From Latin H. of 7th century in Roman Pr. Bk. Lucis Creator optime.

318. **Bread of Heaven.** J. CONDER, 1836.

225. **Brief life.** Rev. J. M. NEALE (1858) from the Latin H. of Bernard of Morlaix, A.D. 1120. Hic breve vivitur, Hic breve plangitur, Hic breve fletur.

161. **Bright the vision.** Bishop MANT, 1837.

412. **Brightly did the.** Dean ALFORD, 1831—1871.

390. **Brightly gleams.** Rev. T. J. POTTER, 1860.

123. **By Jesus' grave.** Rev. I. G. SMITH, 1855.

85. **By precepts taught.** Rev. J. M. NEALE, 1851, and Comps. From St Ambrose or St Gregory. 4th century. Ex more docti mystico.

432. **Captains of the.** Sir H. BAKER, 1861, from Latin Hymn by J. B. Santeuil. Paris Pr. Bk. Cœlestis aulæ principes.

422. **Christ in highest.** Rev. W. PALMER, 1850. From Latin Hymn of J. B. Santeuil. 17th century. Christe qui sedes Olympo.

352. **Christ is gone up.** Rev. J. M. NEALE, 1851.

396, part II. **Christ is made.** Rev. J. M. NEALE, 1851, and Comps. From Latin H. 8th century. Salisbury Pr Bk. Angulare fundamentum.

239. **Christ is our.** Rev. J. CHANDLER, 1841. From a Latin H. 8th century. Angulare fundamentum lapis Christus missus est.

138. **Christ is risen.** Rev. A. GURNEY, 1862.

136. **Christ the Lord.** CATHERINE WINKWORTH, 1858. From a Bohemian H., turned by M. Weiss into German, 1531. Christus ist erstanden.

131. **Christ the Lord is.** J. E. LEESON, 1842. Paris Communion Office. Victimæ paschali laudes.

333. **Christ, who once.** Rev. W. S. BOURNE.

7. **Christ, whose.** Rev. C. WESLEY, 1740.

400. **Christ will gather.** C. WINKWORTH, 1858. From German Hymn by Bp C. Gregor. 18th century. Aller Gläubigen Sammelplatz.

91. **Christian, dost thou.** Rev. J. M. NEALE. From a Greek H. by St Andrew of Crete, A.D. 700. οὐ γὰρ βλέπεις τοὺς ταράττοντας;

269. **Christian, seek.** C. ELLIOTT, 1836.

61. **Christians, awake.** J. Byrom, 1763.
209. **Come, gracious Spirit.** S. Browne, 1720.
347. **Come, Holy Ghost, Creator blest.** Rev. E. Caswall, 1849, and Comps. Latin H. of King Charlemagne, 8th century. Veni Creator Spiritus.
157. **Come, Holy Ghost, our souls.** Bishop Cosin, 17th century. King Charlemagne, A.D. 800. Veni Creator Spiritus.
9. **Come, Holy Ghost, who.** Rev. J. H. Newman, A.D. 1836. From St Ambrose. 4th century.
299. **Come, let us join.** Dr Watts, 1707.
434. **Come, pure hearts.** R. Campbell, 1850, and Comps. Latin H. of Adam of St Victor, 1100. Jucundare plebs fidelis.
139. **Come, see the place.** T. Kelly, 1806, and Comps.
341. **Come, sing with holy gladness.** Rev. J. J. Daniell, 1860.
156. **Come, Thou Holy Spirit, come.** Rev. E. Caswall, 1840, and Comps. Latin H. of King Robert II. A.D. 1000. Veni Sancte Spiritus. "The loveliest of all the sacred Hymns."
256. **Come unto me.** W. C. Dix, 1868.
302. **Come, ye faithful, raise the anthem.** J. Hupton, 1804, and Rev. J. M. Neale, 1853.
133. **Come ye faithful, raise the strain.** Rev. J. M. Neale, 1866. Greek H. of St John Damascene, A.D. 780. ἀσῶμεν πάντες λαοί.
382. **Come, ye thankful.** Dean Alford, 1844.
175. **Conquering kings.** Rev. J. Chandler, 1841, and Comps. From Paris Pr. Bk. Victis sibi cognomina.
45. **Creator of the starry height.** Rev. J. M. Neale, 1851, and Comps. Salisbury Pr. Bk. Conditor alme siderum.
83. **Creator of the world.** Comps. By Coffin, Paris Pr. Bk. Te læta, mundi Conditor.
304. **Crown Him.** M. Bridges, 1848.
398. **Day of wrath.** Rev. W. J. Irons, 1853. Latin of Thomas of Celano, A.D. 1230. Paris Communion Office. Dies iræ, dies illa. "An immortal Hymn of rare merit and world-wide interest."
289. **Days and moments.** Rev. E. Caswall, 1849, and Comps.

420. **Dear Lord, on this.** C. F. Alexander, 1848.
431. **Disposer supreme.** Rev. I. Williams, 1836. Latin Hymn by J. B. Santeuil. 17th century. Paris Pr. Bk. Supreme quales Arbiter.
313. **Draw nigh.** Rev. J. M. Neale, 1853. From a Latin H. in a Monastery at Bangor in Ireland, A. D. 640. A Hymn sung during Holy Communion. Sancti, venite Corpus Christi sumite.

76. **Earth has.** Rev. E. Caswall, 1849, and Comps. From A. C. Prudentius, A.D. 390, (or St Ambrose). O sola magnarum urbium.
370. **Eternal Father.** W. Whiting, 1860.

339. **Fair waved.** Rev. J. H. Gurney, 1838.
284. **Far from my.** Rev. H. F. Lyte, 1834. Psalm 137.
74. **Father, let me dedicate.** Rev. L. Tuttiett, 1870.
275. **Father of all.** Bp Christopher Wordsworth, 1862.
164. **Father of Heaven.** Rev. E Cooper, 1808.
388. **Father of mercies.** A. Flowerdew, 1811.
285. **Fierce raged the.** Rev. G. Thring, 1870. From a Greek H. of St Anatolius, 7th century. ζοφερᾶς τρικυμίας.
65. **First of Martyrs.** Rev. I. Williams, 1840, and Comps. From Latin H., J. B. Santeuil. Paris Pr. Bk. O qui tuo Dux Martyrum.
437. **For all the Saints.** Bp W. W. How, 1864.
418. **For all Thy Saints.** C. F. Alexander, 1848.
461. **For ever we would.** Rev. A. W. Chatfield.
231. **For ever with.** J. Montgomery, 1834.
115. **Forgive them.** C. F. Alexander, 1848.
443. **For man the Saviour.** Rev. I. Williams, 1840, and Comps. By J. B. Santeuil. Paris Pr. Bk. Ex quo salus mortalium.
416. **Forsaken once.** C. F. Alexander, 1848.
227. **For thee, O dear, dear.** Rev. J. M. Neale, 1851. From Latin H. of Bernard of Morlaix, 1150. Oh bona Patria, lumina sobria te speculantur.
448. **For Thy dear Saint.** Bp Mant, 1837.
73. **For Thy mercy.** Rev. H. Downton, 1843.
8. **Forth in Thy.** Rev. C. Wesley, 1749.
92. **Forty days.** Rev. G. Smyttan, 1856, and Rev. F. Pott, 1870.

392. **Forward, be our.** Dean ALFORD, 1831—1871.
358. **From Greenland's icy.** Bp HEBER, 1819.
171. **From highest heaven.** Rev. Sir H. W. BAKER, 1861.
410. **From out the.** C. F. ALEXANDER, 1848.
107. **Glory be.** Rev. E. CASWALL, 1858. From an Italian Hymn, 17th century. Viva viva Gesu.
23. **Glory to Thee.** Bp KEN, 1695.
69. **Glory to Thee, O Lord.** EMMA TOKE, 1853.
3. **Glory to Thee, Who.** Bp KEN, 1695.
110. **Go to dark.** J. MONTGOMERY, 1820.
343. **God Eternal.** Rev. J. E. MILLARD, 1848.
58. **God from on.** Bp WOODFORD, 1851. Paris Pr. Book. C. Coffin, 1736. Jam desinant suspiria.
373. **God moves.** WM. COWPER, 1773, after one of his attacks of mental despair.
364. **God of grace.** Archd. CHURTON, 1854.
218. **God of mercy.** Rev. H. F. LYTE, 1834.
374. **God of our life.** W. COWPER, 1773. In a storm.
385. **God the Father.** Rev. J. M. NEALE, 1851.
26. **God, Who madest.** Bp HEBER, 1827, and Archbp WHATELY, 1855. German Hymn of H. Albert, 1644. Gott des Himmels und der Erden.
89. **Good it is.** Rev. Sir H. BAKER, 1861. From Latin, in Sarum Pr. Bk. Clarum decus jejunii.
342. **Gracious Saviour.** J. E. LEESON, 1842. J. WHITTEMORE, 1860.
210. **Gracious Spirit.** Bp C. WORDSWORTH, 1862.
52. **Great God, what.** W. B. COLLYER, 1812. From German H. of B. RINGWALDT, 1585. Es ist gewisslich an der Zeit dass Gottes Sohn wird kommen.
375. **Great King of nations.** Rev. J. H. GURNEY, 1838.
262. **Great Mover of.** Rev. I. WILLIAMS, 1840. Paris Pr. Bk. C. Coffin. Supreme motor cordium.
196. **Guide me.** W. WILLIAMS, 1760. Written in Welsh.
18. **Hail, gladdening Light.** Rev. J. KEBLE, 1857. From Greek H. of 1st or 2nd century. St Basil says, φῶς ἱλαρον ἁγίας δόξης. Evening H. of the Greek Ch.
147. **Hail the day.** Rev. C. WESLEY, 1739. Cp. Fortunatus. Sung by Jerome of Prague at the stake, and translated by Cranmer. Salve festa dies toto venerabilis ævo.

219. **Hail to the Lord's.** J. MONTGOMERY, 1831. Psalm 72.
47. **Hark! a thrilling voice.** Rev. E. CASWALL, 1849, and Comps. From St Ambrose :
En! clara vox redarguit
Vox clara Ecce! intonat—5th century.
223. **Hark! hark! my soul.** Rev. F. W. FABER, 1852.
260. **Hark! my soul.** W. COWPER, 1769—1779.
53. **Hark! the glad sound.** Dr DODDRIDGE, 1735.
60. **Hark! the herald.** Rev. C. WESLEY (1758) and M. MADAN (1760). Cp. St Cosmas (760). "Χριστὸς γεννᾶται δοξάσετε."
436. **Hark! the sound.** Bp C. WORDSWORTH, 1862.
249. **Have mercy, Lord.** N. TATE and N. BRADY, 1700, from Psalm 51.
162. **Have mercy on us.** Rev. F. W. FABER, 1852.
338. **Heavenly Father.** Bp C. WORDSWORTH, 1862.
462. **Herald in the.** Dean ALFORD, 1860.
102. **He Who once.** Rev. E. CASWALL, 1849, and Comps. From Latin H. of 17th century. Roman Pr. Bk. Ira justa conditoris.
119. **His are the.** C. F. ALEXANDER, 1848.
22. **Holy Father.** Rev. R. H. ROBINSON, 1869.
148. **Holy Ghost.** Bp C. WORDSWORTH, 1862.
160. **Holy, Holy, Holy.** Bp HEBER, 1811.
241. **Hosanna to the.** Bp HEBER, 1811.
340. **Hosanna we sing.** Rev. G. S. HODGES, 1870.
357. **How blessed.** From Hymns from the Land of Luther, by Miss JANE BORTHWICK, 1853, from German of Spitta, 1833. O hochbeglückte Seele.
457. **How blest.** Comps. from Latin of Sylvius. Roman Pr. Bk. Fortem virili pectore.
438. **How bright.** Dr WATTS, 1709, and W. CAMERON, 1781.
404. **How oft.** Rev. W. BRIGHT, 1868.
176. **How sweet.** Rev. J. NEWTON, 1779.
75. **How vain.** Rev. J. M. NEALE, 1851, and Comps. from Latin H. Cp. Illuxit orbi jam dies.
351. **How welcome.** Sir H. BAKER, 1861.
323. **I am not worthy.** Sir H. BAKER, 1861.
186. **I could not.** F. R. HAVERGAL, 1859.
257. **I heard the voice.** Dr H. BONAR, 1850.
330. **I love to hear the story.** E. H. MILLER.

189. **Jesu, Thy mercies.** Rev. E. Caswall, 1840. Latin of St Bernard of Clairvaux, 12th century. Amor, Jesu! dulcissimus.

455. **Jesu, the Virgin's.** Rev. J. M. Neale, 1851, and Comps. From date of St Ambrose, 4th century. Jesu, corona virginum.

403. **Jesus calls.** C. F. Alexander, 1853.

134. **Jesus Christ.** Author unknown. C. B. in 1708, from Latin H. of 15th century. Christus hodie resurrexit.

170. **Jesus is God.** Rev. F. W. Faber, 1862.

287. **Jesus, Lord.** J. Cummins, 1849.

140. **Jesus lives.** F. E. Cox, 1841. From German of C. Gellert, 1757. Jesus lebt, mit ihm auch ich.

220. **Jesus shall.** Dr Watts, 1719. Translation of Psalm 72.

153. **Joy! because.** Rev. J. Ellerton, 1870, and Rev. F. Hort, from Latin H. of 7th century. Beata nobis gaudia.

255. **Just as I am.** C. Elliott, 1836.

419. **King of Saints.** Rev. J. Ellerton, 1871.

266. **Lead, kindly.** Rev. J. H. Newman (1833). Written in Straits of Bonifacio.

281. **Lead us.** J. Edmeston, 1821.

441. **Let our Choir.** Rev. J. M. Neale, 1860. From Greek of St Joseph, 9th century. τῶν ἱερῶν ἀθλοφόρων.

221. **Let saints.** Rev. C. Wesley, 1740.

397. **Lift the strain.** Rev. J. Ellerton, 1869.

126. **Light's glittering.** Rev. J. M. Neale, 1851, and Comps. From Latin of St Ambrose. 4th century. Aurora lucis rutilat.

232. **Light's abode.** Rev. J. M. Neale, 1851, and Comps. From Latin of Roman Pr. Bk. Jerusalem luminosa. Cp. "Urbs beata Hierusalem" and "Cœlestis urbs Jerusalem."

414. **Lo from the.** Rev. I. Williams, 1840. From Latin H. of C. Coffin, 1700. Nunc suis tandem novus e latebris.

51. **Lo! He comes.** Rev. C. Wesley, 1758.

88. **Lo! now.** Rev. J. M. Neale, 1851, and Comps. From Latin of St Gregory, 6th century. Salisbury Pr. Bk. Ecce tempus idoneum.

435. **Lo! round.** R. HILL, 1790, and others. Mary L. Duncan? 1830.
310. **Lo! the angels'.** Comps. from Latin. Ecce panis angelorum.
267. **Lord, as.** Rev. J. H. GURNEY, 1838.
362. **Lord, her.** Rev. H. DOWNTON, 1867.
 94. **Lord, in this Thy.** Rev. ISAAC WILLIAMS, 1840, from "The Baptistery." Image 20th.
143. **Lord in Thy.** Rev. J. KEBLE, 1856.
185. **Lord Jesus.** Rev. A. W. CHATFIELD.
344. **Lord Jesus, God and Man.** Sir H. BAKER, 1861.
367. **Lord of glory.** E. S. ALDERSON, 1860.
214. **Lord of our life.** By PHILIP PUSEY. From H. of 8th century. From Salisbury Hymn Book, 1857.
387. **Lord of the harvest.** PROFESSOR J. ANSTICE, 1836.
356. **Lord, speak.** F. R. HAVERGAL, 1859.
355. **Lord, pour Thy.** J. MONTGOMERY, 1825.
247. **Lord, teach us how.** J. MONTGOMERY, 1825.
243. **Lord, Thy Word.** Rev. SIR H. BAKER, 1861.
116. **Lord, when Thy.** Bp W. D. MACLAGAN, 1870.
244. **Lord, when we.** Rev. J. D. CARLYLE (1802).
334. **Loving Shepherd.** JANE E. LEESON, 1842.
 33. **Morn of morns.** Rev. I. WILLIAMS, 1840, and Comps. From Latin H., 18th century. Paris Pr. Bk. Die dierum principe.
  5. **My Father.** SIR H. BAKER, 1861.
349. **My God, accept.** M. BRIDGES, 1848.
317. **My God, and.** Dr DODDRIDGE, 1755.
169. **My God, how.** Rev. F. W. FABER, 1862.
106. **My God, I love Thee.** Rev. E. CASWALL, 1849, and Comps. From Latin of St Francis Xavier, 16th century. O Deus ego amo Te.
264. **My God, my Father.** CHARLOTTE ELLIOTT, 1834.
277. **Nearer, my God.** Mrs S. F. ADAMS, 1840.
  4. **New every.** Rev. J. KEBLE, 1822.
 41. **New wonders.** Rev. J. CHANDLER, and Comps. from Latin H. by Coffin, 18th century (Paris Pr. Bk.) Miramur O Deus tuae.
451. **Not by the.** Rev. I. WILLIAMS, 1840, and Comps. From Latin H. by J. B. SANTEUIL, 17th century. Paris Pr. Bk. Non parta solo sanguine.
103. **Now, my soul.** Sir H. BAKER and Rev. J. CHANDLER. From C. H. SANTEUIL. Paris Pr. Bk. Prome vocem mens canoram.

309. **Now my tongue.** Rev. E. CASWALL and Comps. From Latin of St Thomas Aquinas, 1270. Pange lingua gloriosi corporis mysterium.

379 **Now thank.** C. WINKWORTH, 1858. From German of M. Rinckart, 1644. The German National H. Nun danket alle Gott.

1. **Now that the daylight fills the sky.** Rev. J. M. NEALE, and Comps. From Latin of St Ambrose, 4th century. Jam lucis orto sidere.

16. **Now that the daylight dies away.** Rev. J. H. NEWMAN. From Latin of St Ambrose, 4th century. Te lucis ante terminum.

346. **Now the day is over.** Rev. S. BARING-GOULD, 1865.

401. **Now the labourer's.** Rev. J. ELLERTON, 1871.

97. **Now the thirty.** Rev. J. M. NEALE and Comps. From Latin of Fortunatus, 6th century. Pange lingua gloriosi prælium certaminis. Cp. Crux benedicta nitet Dominus qua carne pependit.

71. **O blessed day.** Rev. J. CHANDLER, 1841, and Comps. From Latin H., Paris Pr. Bk., by Abbé Besnault, 17th century. Felix dies quam proprio.

145. **O Christ our joy.** D. T. MORGAN, 1862. From Latin. Tu Christe nostrum gaudium.

57. **O Christ, Redeemer.** Sir H. BAKER, 1861, from Latin H. of 6th century. Salisbury Pr. Bk. Christe Redemptor omnium.

129. **O Christ, the heavens'.** Comps. Roman Pr. Bk. Rex sempiterne cœlitum.

95. **O Christ, who.** Rev. J. W. COPELAND and Comps. From Latin H., Salisbury Pr. Bk. Christe qui Lux es et Dies.

59. **O come all.** Rev. F. OAKELEY and Comps. from Latin H., Salisbury Pr. Bk., 15th century. Adeste fideles læti triumphantes.

114. **O come, and.** Rev. F. W. FABER, 1862.

49. **O come, O come.** Rev. J. M. NEALE, 1851, and Comps. From Latin H. (French Communion Service). From the Antiphons commonly called the O's. Veni, veni, Emmanuel.

55. **O come, Redeemer.** D. T. MORGAN. St Ambrose, 4th century. Veni, Redemptor gentium. "An immortal heritage of the Universal Church."

36. **O day of rest.** Bp C. WORDSWORTH, 1862.

29. **O Father.** Rev. H. B. HEATHCOTE, 1850.

325. **O Father, Thou.** C. WINKWORTH, 1862. German of
A. KNAPP, 19th century. O Vaterherz das Erd
und Himmel schuf.
314. **O food that.** Comps. From Latin.
278. **O for a faith.** Rev. W. H. BATHURST, 1842.
11. **O God of all.** Rev. J. M. NEALE, 1859, and Comps.
From Latin of St Ambrose, 4th century. Rerum
Deus tenax vigor.
237. **O God of hosts.** N TATE and N. BRADY, 1696.
376. **O God of love.** Sir H. BAKER, 1861.
10. **O God of truth.** Rev. J. M. NEALE, 1859. Comps.
From St Ambrose, 4th century. Rector potens
verax Deus.
442. **O God, Thy soldiers'.** Rev. J. M. NEALE, 1859, and
Comps. From St Ambrose, 4th century. Deus
tuorum militum.
165. **O God, our help.** Dr WATTS, 1719. From 90th
Psalm by Moses.
320. **O God, unseen.** E. OSLER, 1837.
224. **O happy band.** Rev. J. M. NEALE, 1866. From
Greek of St Joseph, 9th century.
429. **O heavenly Jerusalem.** Rev. I. WILLIAMS, 1840.
From Latin, Paris Pr. Bk. Cœlestis O Jerusalem.
46. **O heavenly Word.** Comps. From Latin. Salisbury
Pr. Bk. Verbum supernum prodiens.
279. **O help us, Lord.** Dean MILMAN, 1837.
211. **O Holy Ghost.** Sir H. BAKER, 1861.
208. **O Holy Spirit.** Rev. J. CHANDLER, 1841. Comps
From Latin. Paris Pr. Bk. O Fons amoris Spiritus.
253. **O Jesu Christ.** Rev. E. CASWALL, 1849.
178, part II. **O Jesu, King.** Rev. E. CASWALL, and Comps.
From Latin, St Bernard of Clairvaux, 12th century.
Jesu rex admirabilis.
2. **O Jesu, Lord.** Rev. J. CHANDLER, 1841, and Comps.
From St Ambrose, 4th century. Splendor paternæ
gloriæ.
178, part III. **O Jesu, Thou.** Rev. E. CASWALL and Comps.
From St Bernard of Clairvaux, 12th century. Jesu
decus angelicum.
198. **O Jesu, Thou art.** Bp W. W. HOW, 1866.
271. **O Jesus, I.** Rev. J. E. BODE, 1869.
456. **O Lamb of God.** Rev. V. S. S. COLES, 1870.
286. **O let him.** F. E. Cox, 1841. From German. H. S.
OSWALD, 1793. Wenn in Leidenstagen.

345. O Light. Dean PLUMPTRE, 1865.
276. O Lord, how happy. J. ANSTICE, 1836.
273. O Lord, how joyful Rev. J. CHANDLER, 1841. From Latin. By J. B. SANTEUIL, 17th century. Paris Pr. Bk. O quam juvat fratres Deus.
365. O Lord of heaven. Bp C. WORDSWORTH, 1863.
394. O Lord of hosts. Rev. J. M. NEALE, 1851.
144. O Lord most High. Rev. J. M. NEALE, and Comps. From St Ambrose, 4th century. Æterne rex altissime.
93. O Lord, turn. J. MARDLEY or J. MARCHANT, 1562.
195. O Love Divine. Rev. C. WESLEY, 1749.
173. O Love, how deep. Rev. J. M. NEALE, and Comps. From Latin H. of 16th century. O Amor quam exstaticus.
192. O Love, who. C. WINKWORTH, 1858. From German of Scheffler, 1650. Liebe, die du mich zum Bilde.
87. O merciful Creator, Rev. J. M. NEALE, and Comps. From Latin of St Gregory, 6th century, or St Ambrose, 4th century. Audi benigne Conditor.
234. O Paradise. Rev. F. W. FABER, 1862.
120. O perfect life of love. Sir H. BAKER, 1861.
380. O praise our God. Sir H. BAKER.
294. O praise our great. H. AUBER, 1829.
308. O praise ye. Sir H. BAKER, 1861.
204. O quickly. Rev. L. TUTTIETT, 1868.
111. O sacred Head. Sir H. BAKER. From Latin. St Bernard of Clairvaux, 12th century. Salve caput cruentatum. Cp. O Haupt voll Blut und Wunden. P. Gerhardt.
311, part II. O saving Victim. Rev. J. CASWALL, and Comps. From Latin H. of 14th century. Verbum procedens a Patre.
272. O Saviour. Rev. W. H. BATHURST, 1842.
63. O Saviour Lord. Rev. J. W. COPELAND, 1848, and Comps. From Latin H. of 15th century. Salisbury Pr. Bk. Salvator mundi Domine.
307. O Saviour, precious. F. R. HAVERGAL, 1859.
146. O Saviour, who. Rev. J. CHANDLER, 1841, and Comps. From Paris Pr. Bk., by Coffin, 18th century. Opus peregisti tuum.
453. O Shepherd. Rev. S. S. COLES.
104. O sinner. Rev. J. M. NEALE, and Comps. From Latin H. of 17th century. (Mozarabic Pr. Bk.)

407. **O Sion.** Rev. E. Caswall, 1849. From Latin. J. B. Santeuil. Paris Pr. Bk. Templi sacratas pande Sion fores.
413. **O Son of God.** Rev. J. Ellerton, 1871.
130. **O sons and daughters.** Rev. J. M. Neale, 1851, and Comps. From Latin H. of 12th century (or St Ambrose). O filii et filiæ.
12. **O Strength and Stay.** Rev. J. Ellerton, and Dr Hort, 1870. From Latin Ambrosian H. Rerum Deus tenax vigor.
283. **O Thou from.** Rev. J. Haweis, 1800.
452. **O Thou whose.** Rev. R. M. Benson. From a Latin H. of 9th century. Roman Pr. Bk.
86. **O Thou who.** Rev. J. M. Hewett, 1859, and Comps, From Latin H., Stuttgart Pr. Bk. Summi largitor præmii.
353. **O Thou who makest.** Bp Armstrong, 1847.
14. **O Trinity.** Rev. J. M. Neale, 1851, and Comps. From Latin of St Gregory, 6th century, or St Ambrose, 4th century. O Lux beata Trinitas.
395. **O Word of God.** Rev. I. Williams, 1840, and Comps. from Latin by Guiet, 17th century. Paris Pr. Bk. Patris æterni soboles coæva.
167. **O worship.** Sir R. Grant, 1839. Psalm 104.
101. **O'erwhelmed.** Rev. E. Caswall, 1849, and Comps. From Latin H. of 17th century. Roman Pr. Bk. Sævo dolorum turbine.
56. **Of the Father's.** Rev. J. M. Neale, 1851. Sir H. Baker, from Latin H. of Prudentius, 4th century. Hereford Pr. Bk. Corde natus ex parentis.
291. **Oft in danger.** H. Kirke White and others, 1827.
446. **Oh what if.** Sir H. Baker, 1861.
235. **Oh what the joy.** Rev. J. M. Neale, 1851, and Comps. From Latin H. of 13th century. O quanta qualia sunt illa sabbata.
50. **On Jordan's bank.** Rev. J. Chandler, 1841, and Comps. Latin H., Paris Pr. Bk. Jordanis oras prævia.
372. **On the waters.** W. C. Dix, 1867.
34. **On this day.** Sir H. Baker, 1861. From Latin, Le Mans Pr. Bk. Die parente temporum. Cp. Primo dierum omnium, of St Gregory.
329. **Once in royal.** C. F. Alexander, 1848.

84. **Once more the.** Rev. J. CHANDLER, 1841. Comps. From Latin H. by Coffin,18th century. Paris Pr. Bk. Sollemne nos jejunii.

315. **Once, only once.** Rev. W. BRIGHT, 1868.

391. **Onward.** Rev. S. BARING-GOULD, 1865.

207. **Our blest Redeemer.** H. AUBER, 1829.

30. **Our day of praise.** Rev. J. ELLERTON, 1867.

250. **Out of the deep I call.** Sir H. BAKER, 1861.

445. **Palms of glory.** JAMES MONTGOMERY, 1819.

240. **Pleasant are Thy.** Rev. H. F. LYTE, 1834. Ps. 84.

298. **Praise, my soul.** Rev. H. F. LYTE. Ps. 103.

381. **Praise, O praise.** Sir H. BAKER. Ps. 136.

292. **Praise the Lord.** Rev. J. KEMPTHORNE ? J. J. Schütz, 17th century. Sei Lob und Ehr dem höchsten Gott.

421. **Praise to God.** Rev. R. M. BENSON, 1861.

172. **Praise to the Holiest.** Rev. J. H. NEWMAN. From the dream of Gerontius, 1865. The 5th choir of Angelicals.

409. **Praise we the Lord.** H. FALLOW's Selection, 1847.

202. **Rejoice, the.** Rev. C. WESLEY, 1748.

378. **Rejoice to-day.** Sir H. BAKER, 1861, from Ps. 98.

393. **Rejoice ye.** Dean PLUMPTRE, 1868.

124. **Resting from.** Rev. J. WHYTEHEAD, 1840.

99. **Ride on.** Dean MILMAN, 1827.

184. **Rock of.** Rev. A. M. TOPLADY, 1775. The Prince Consort repeated this H. when dying.

151. **Ruler of.** Rev. J. CHANDLER, 1841, and Comps. From Latin H., Paris Pr. Bk. Supreme Rector cœlitum.

31. **Saviour, again.** Rev. J. ELLERTON, 1866.

305. **Saviour, blessed.** Rev. E. THRING, 1862.

359. **Saviour, sprinkle.** Bp COXE, 1851.

251. **Saviour, when.** Sir R. GRANT, 1815.

148. **See the Conqueror.** Bp C. WORDSWORTH, 1862.

113. **See the destined.** Bp MANT, 1837. From Latin H. of St Ambrose, 4th century, or Fortunatus, 6th century. Lustra sex qui jam peregit.

450. **Shall we not love thee.** Sir H. BAKER, 1861.

248. **Shepherd divine.** Rev. C. WESLEY, 1748.

296. **Sing Alleluia.** Rev. J. ELLERTON, 1865. From Latin H. of 8th century. Mozarabic Pr. Bk. Alleluia ! piis edite laudibus.

97. **Sing, my.** Rev. J. M. Neale, 1851, and Comps. From Latin H. of Fortunatus, 6th century. Pange lingua gloriosi prælium certaminis. Cp. Crux benedicta nitet Dominus qua carne pependit.

293. **Sing praise.** F. E. Cox, 1864. From German H. of J. J. Schütz, 1673. Sei Lob und Ehr dem höchsten Gott.

39. **Sing we the.** Rev. J. Chandler, 1841, and Comps. From Latin.

100. **Sion's daughter.** Sir H. Baker, 1861. From Latin H., Roman Pr. Bk. Venit e cælo mediator alto.

44. **Six days of.** Rev. J. Chandler, 1841, and Comps. From Latin by Coffin, 18th century. Paris Pr. Bk. Tandem peractis O Deus.

270. **Soldiers of Christ.** Rev. C. Wesley, 1749.

447. **Soldiers who are.** Rev. J. H. Clark. From Latin H. in Paris Pr. Bk. Pugnate Christi milites.

459. **Son of the Highest.** Rev. E. Caswall, 1849, and Comps. Roman Pr. Bk. Summi parentis unice.

297. **Songs of praise.** J. Montgomery, 1819.

81. **Songs of thankfulness.** Bp. C. Wordsworth, 1862.

155. **Spirit of mercy.** From Foundling Hospital Collection, 1774.

423. **Stars of the morning.** Rev. J. M. Neale, 1866. From Greek H. of St Joseph, 9th century.

24. **Sun of my soul.** Rev. J. Keble, 1820.

68. **Sweet flowerets.** Sir H. Baker, 1861. Cp. Prudentius, 390 A.D. Salvete flores martyrum.

28. **Sweet Saviour.** Rev. F. W. Faber, 1852.

109. **Sweet the moments.** J. Allen, 1757, and Hon. and Rev. W. Shirley, 1774.

263. **Take up thy.** C. W. Everest, 1833.

402. **Tender Shepherd.** C. Winkworth, 1858. From German H. of Meinhold, 1797. Guter Hirt, Du hast gestillt.

222. **Ten thousand.** Dean Alford, 1850.

206. **That day of wrath.** Sir W. Scott, 1805, in Lay of Last Minstrel, from St Thomas of Celano, 13th century. Dies iræ, dies illa.

126, part III. **That Eastertide.** Rev. J. M. Neale, 1851, and Comps. From Latin of St Ambrose, 4th century. Claro Paschali gaudio.

48. **The Advent.** Rev. J. Chandler, 1841, and Comps.

From Latin H. by Coffin, 18th century. Instantis adventum Dei.

70. **The ancient law departs.** Comps. From Latin H. by Besnault, 18th century. Paris Pr. Bk.

126, part ii. **The Apostles' hearts.** Rev. J. M. NEALE, and Comps. From Latin of St Ambrose, 4th century. Tristes erant Apostoli.

215. **The Church's one.** Rev. S. J. STONE, 1865.

132. **The day of.** Rev. J. M. NEALE, 1866. Greek of St John Damascene, 8th century. ἀναστάσεως ἡμέρα.

21. **The day is.** Rev. J. M. NEALE. From Greek of St Anatolius, 5th century. τὴν ἡμέραν διελθών. A favourite H. in the Greek Isles.

354. **The earth, O Lord.** Rev. J. M. NEALE, 1851.

430. **The eternal gifts.** Rev. J. M. NEALE. Comps. From Latin H. of St Ambrose, 4th century. Æterna Christi munere, Apostolorum gloria.

42. **The fish in wave.** Rev. J. CHANDLER, 1841, and Comps. Latin H. (Paris Pr. Bk.) by Coffin. Iisdem creati fluctibus.

449. **The God whom earth.** Rev. J. M. NEALE, and Comps. From Latin of Fortunatus, 6th century. Quem terra pontus æthera.

415. **The Great.** Rev. J. M. NEALE, 1851. Latin H. of Venerable Bede, 8th century. Precursor altus Luminis.

301. **The Head that.** T. KELLY, 1804.

78. **The Heavenly Child.** Rev. J. CHANDLER, 1841, and Comps. From Latin (Paris Pr. Bk.) by J. B. Santeuil, 17th century. Divine crescebas puer.

311. **The Heavenly Word.** Rev. J. M. NEALE, and Comps. From Latin H. of St Thomas Aquinas. Pr. Bk. of 14th century,
> Verbum procedens a Patre
> Verbum supernum prodiens.

197. **The King of love.** Sir H. BAKER, 1861, from Ps. 23, and his last dying words.

128. **The Lamb's high.** Rev. J. M. NEALE, 1851. Comps. From Latin H. of St Ambrose of 7th century (Salisbury Pr. Bk.) Ad cœnam Agni providi.

66. **The life which.** Rev. E. CASWALL, 1840, and Comps. From Latin H. (Cluniac Pr. Bk.) Quæ dixit, egit, pertulit.

80. The people that. J. MORRISON, 1780.
19. The radiant morn. Rev. E. THRING, 1866.
229. The roseate hues. C. F. ALEXANDER, 1848.
96. The royal banners. Rev. J. M. NEALE, 1851, and Comps. From Latin H. of Fortunatus, 6th century. Vexilla Regis prodeunt. One of the grandest Hymns of the Latin Church.
428. The Saints of God. Bp MACLAGAN, 1870.
405. The Shepherd now. Rev. F. POTT, and Comps. From Latin H. (Paris Pr. Bk., by De Geste, 18th century). Pastore percusso, minas.
295. The strain upraise. Rev. J. M. NEALE. From the Latin of Godescalcus, 10th century. Stuttgart Pr. Bk. Cantemus cuncti melodum nunc alleluia. Cp. Ps. 148. "A world-famous sequence."
439. The Son of God. Bp HEBER, 1827. Cp. the Greek of St Anatolius, 5th century. τῷ βασιλεῖ καὶ δεσπότῃ.
386. The Sower. Rev. W. St H. BOURNE.
135. The strife. Rev. F. POTTS, and Comps. From Latin H. of 12th century. Finita jam sunt prælia.
17. The sun. Rev. E. CASWALL, 1849. From Latin H. Sol præceps rapitur proxima nox est.
350. The voice. Rev. J. KEBLE, 1857.
226. The world is. Rev. J. M. NEALE. From Latin H. of Bernard of Morlaix, 12th century. Hora novissima, tempora pessima sunt, Vigilemus.
72. The year is. The Rev. F. POTTS and Comps. From Latin H., Meaux Pr. Bk. Lapsus est annus, redit annus alter.
312. Thee we adore. Bp WOODFORD, 1852. From Latin H. of St Thomas Aquinas, 13th century. Adoro te devote latens Deitas.
230. There is a blessed. Sir H. BAKER, 1861.
168. There is a book. Rev. J. KEBLE, 1819.
332. There is a green hill. C. F. ALEXANDER, 1848.
411. There is one way. C. F. ALEXANDER.
337. There is a friend. A. MIDLANE, 1860.
424. They come. R. CAMPBELL, 1850.
369. Thine arm. Dean E. H. PLUMPTRE, 1865.
280. Thine for ever. M. F. MAUDE, 1848.
37. This is the day. Rev. J. ELLERTON, 1868.
203. Thou art coming. F. R. HAVERGAL, 1859.
149. Thou art gone up. E. TOKE, 1853.

417. **Thou art the Christ.** Bp W. W. How, 1871.
199. **Thou art the Way.** Bp Doane, 1824.
205. **Thou Judge.** Rev. C. Wesley, 1749.
 40. **Thou spakest.** Rev. I. Williams, and Comps. From Latin of Coffin, 18th century.
368. **Thou to Whom.** Rev. G. Thring, 1870.
426. **Thou Who sentest.** Rev. J. Ellerton, 1871.
360. **Thou Whose.** Rev. J. Marriott, 1813.
163. **Three in One.** Rev. G. Rorison, 1849. Cp. St Ambrose, 4th century. O Lux beata Trinitas.
118. **Throned.** Rev. J. Ellerton, 1871.
290. **Through all.** N. Tate and N. Brady, 1696. From Psalm 34.
361. **Through midnight.** Rev. S. J. Stone, 1865.
 25. **Through the day.** T. Kelly, 1806.
274. **Through the night.** Rev. S. Baring-Gould, 1867. From the Danish H. of Ingemann, 1825. Igjennem Nat og Trængsel.
217. **Thy kingdom come.** Rev. L. Hensley.
259. **Thy life was given for me.** F. R. Havergal.
265. **Thy way, not mine.** Dr H. Bonar, 1857.
327. **'Tis done.** Sir H. Baker, 1861.
180. **To Christ.** Rev. E. Caswall, 1849. Comps. From Latin H., Roman Pr. Bk. Summi Parentis Filio.
179. **To the Name.** Rev. J. M. Neale, 1851, and Comps. From Latin H. of 15th century. Liege Pr. Bk. Gloriosi Salvatoris.
212. **To Thee.** F. R. Havergal, 1859.
384. **To Thee, O Lord.** W. C. Dix.
142. **To Thee, our God.** Bp W. W. How, 1871.
 43. **To-day, O Lord.** Rev. J. Chandler, 1841, and Comps. From Latin H., Paris Pr. Bk., by Coffin, 18th century. Jam sanctius moves opus.
331. **We are but.** C. F. Alexander, 1848.
366. **We give Thee.** Bp W. W. How, 1854.
181. **We know Thee.** Rev. W. Bright.
242. **We love the place.** Rev. W. Bullock, 1854, and Sir H. Baker, 1860.
383. **We plough the fields.** Miss J. M. Campbell, 1861. From German of M. Claudius, 1782. Wir pflügen und wir streuen.
321. **We pray Thee.** Rev. V. S. S. Coles.
174. **We saw Thee not.** Rev. J. H. Gurney, 1851.

406. **We sing the.** Rev. J. ELLERTON, 1871.
200. **We sing the praise.** T. KELLY, 1815, and Comps.
252. **Weary of earth.** Rev. S. J. STONE, 1865.
389. **What our Father.** Sir H. BAKER, 1861, and Comps.
   From German of Schmolke, 1720. Cp. Rodigast,
   Was Gott thut das ist wohl gethan.
 77. **What star is this?** Rev. J. CHANDLER, 1841, and
   Comps. From Latin H. of Coffin, 18th century.
   Paris Pr. Bk. Quae stella sole pulchrior.
425. **What thanks and praise.** Bp MACLAGAN.
216. **What time the.** Rev. J. W. HEWETT, 1855.
246. **What various.** W. COWPER, 1779.
245. **When at Thy.** Rev. H. F. LYTE, 1845.
154. **When God of old.** Rev. J. KEBLE, 1822.
108. **When I survey.** Dr WATTS, 1707, and Comps.
303. **When morning gilds.** Rev. E. CASWALL, 1849.
   From Latin H.
399. **When our heads.** Dean MILMAN, 1827.
 54. **When shades of night.** Comps. From Latin H.
   Paris Pr. Bk. In noctis umbra desides.
183. **When wounded sore.** C. F. ALEXANDER, 1848.
201. **Where high the.** M. BRUCE, 1767.
 62. **While shepherds watched.** N. TATE, 1696.
427. **Who are these.** F. E. Cox, 1841. From German of
   T. Schenk, 18th century. Wer sind die vor Gottes
   Throne.
159. **With hearts renewed.** D. T. MORGAN. From the
   Latin.
326. **Within the.** K. D. CORNISH.
 67. **Word Supreme.** Rev. J. KEBLE, from Salisbury H.
   Bk., 1856.
125. **Ye Choirs of.** R. CAMPBELL, 1850, and Comps. From
   Latin H. of St Fulbert, 1020. Chorus novæ
   Jerusalem.
444. **Ye servants of our glorious King.** R. CAMPBELL,
   and Comps. From Latin H. of St Ambrose, 4th
   century. Æterna Christi munera.
268. **Ye servants of the Lord.** Dr DODDRIDGE, 1755.
 64. **Yesterday, with exultation.** Rev. J. M. NEALE,
   1851, and Comps. From Latin of Adam of St
   Victor, 12th century. Heri mundus exultavit.

LITANIES.

INDEX TO GREEK FIRST LINES.

LATIN FIRST LINES.

97. Pange lingua gloriosi prælium certaminis.
405. Pastore percusso minas.
395. Patris æterni soboles coæva.
415. Precursor altus Luminis.
 34. Primo dierum omnium.
103. Prome vocem mens canoram.
447. Pugnate Christi milites.
 66. Quæ dixit, egit, pertulit.
 77. Quæ stella sole pulchrior.
449. Quem terra pontus æthera.
112. Quicumque certum quæritis.
 10. Rector potens verax Deus.
 11. Rerum Deus tenax vigor.
 12. Rerum Deus tenax vigor.
129. Rex sempiterne cœlitum.
 63. Salvator mundi Domine.
111. Salve caput cruentatum.
147. Salve festa dies toto venerabilis ævo.
 68. Salvete flores martyrum.
313. Sancti, venite Corpus Christi sumite.
101. Sævo dolorum turbine.
 84. Sollemne nos jejunii.
 17. Sol præceps rapitur, proxima nox est.
  2. Splendor paternæ gloriæ.
117. Stabat mater dolorosa.
180. Summi Parentis Filio.
 86. Summi largitor præmii.
459. Summi parentis unice.
151. Supreme Rector cœlitum.
431. Supreme quales Arbiter.
262. Supreme motor cordium.
134. Surrexit Christus hodie.
 44. Tandem peractis O Deus.
 83. Te læta, mundi Conditor.
 15. Te lucis ante terminum.
 16. Te lucis ante terminum.
407. Templi sacratas pande Sion fores.
126, part II. Tristes erant Apostoli.
145. Tu Christe nostrum gaudium.
232. Urbs beata Hierusalem.
396. Urbs beata Hierusalem.
228. Urbs Sion aurea patria lactea.
311. Verbum procedens a Patre.

46. Verbum supernum prodiens.
311. Verbum supernum prodiens.
49. Veni, veni, Emmanuel.
157. Veni Creator Spiritus.
347. Veni Creator Spiritus.
55. Veni, Redemptor gentium.
156. Veni Sancte Spiritus.
100. Venit e cælo mediator alto.
96. Vexilla Regis prodeunt.
131. Victimæ paschali laudes.
175. Victis sibi cognomina.
47. Vox clara ecce intonat.

See 39, 40, 159, 303, 311, part II., 314, First Lines wanting
and Names of Authors.

GERMAN FIRST LINES.

27. Ach bleib mit deiner Gnade.
400. Aller Gläubigen Sammelplatz.
136. Christus ist erstanden.
52. Es ist gewisslich an der Zeit Dass Gottes Sohn wird
    kommen.
26. Gott des Himmels und der Erden.
402. Guter Hirt, du hast gestillt.
140. Jesus lebt, mit ihm auch ich.
192. Liebe, die du mich zum Bilde.
379. Nun danket alle Gott.
111. O Haupt voll Blut und Wunden.
357. O hochbeglückte Seele.
325. O Vaterherz das Erd und Himmel schuf.
292. ⎫
293. ⎭ Sei Lob und Ehr dem höchsten Gott.
389. Was Gott thut das ist wohl gethan.
286. Wenn in Leidenstagen.
427. Wer sind die vor Gottes Throne.
383. Wir pflügen und wir streuen.

ITALIAN FIRST LINE.

107. Viva viva Gesu.

DANISH FIRST LINE.

274. Igjennem Nat og Trængsel.

HARD WORDS MADE CLEARER.

Absorbing, H. 1. Swallowing up. Engaging wholly.

Abstinence, H. 87, 90. Eating no food. Fasting is change of food.

Acclaim, H. 432. Shout together.

Affray, H. 97. A fearful fight.

Alloy, H. 28. A base mixture.

Alpha and Omega, H. 313. Revelation i. 8. First and last letters of Greek Alphabet. The whole.

Amber, H. 410. Yellow.

Antiphons, H. 296. Responsive Hymns sung in parts.

Arraigned, H. 110. Accused, H. 398. To seek reasons for.

Attesting, H. 113. Able to bear witness. 216.

Beatific, H. 226. The sight of their Saviour. H. 436. The blessed Sight.

Behests, H. 422. Commands.

Benign, H. 77. Benignant, kind. 163.

Blazon, H. 328. To adorn.

Blending, H. 12. Mingling.

Boding, H. 251. Foreboding. Foretelling the destruction.

Bonded, H. 227. Built together. Bound.

Canopy, H. 167. Covering.

Canticles, H. 33. Short Psalms and Hymns. H. 303.

Chalice, H. 197. The Cup in Holy Communion. H. 395.

Chaos, H. 360. Confusion. The void earth, Gen. i. 2.

Charter, H. 215. Her "Magna Charta." Her Bill of Rights. Her foundation claim.

Co-Eternal, H. 302. Of the same eternal nature. Each everlasting.

Consubstantial, H. 302. Of the same substance.

Consummation, H. 215. The full bestowal of.

Converse, H. 3. Conversation. Manner of Life.

Convocations, H. 36. Assemblies. Meetings.

Cope, H. 225. The Church must struggle with the world.

Descries, H. 67. Perceives. Sees.

Diadem, H. 253. Crown. H. 254.

Dominations, H. 306. Ranks of Angels.
Dower, H. 227. Gift. H. 365.

Efface, H. 88. Wipe out—do away.
Enable, H. 157. Make able, strengthen.
Enthral, H. 127. Make a slave of—Enslave. H. 140, 204.
Epiphany, H. 75. Manifestation. Revealing.
Eucharistic, H. 316. Thanksgiving. The Holy Communion. 321. Praise.
Exile, H. 458. Driven from home into a strange land.

Fane, H. 425. Sacred Building.
Fell, H. 377. Cruel.
Foil, H. 27. Baffle—beat—make foolish.

Garish, H. 266. Staring. Glaring.
Gradation, H. 12. Steps. Order.
Guerdon, H. 254. A gift back—reward. H. 460.

Haled, H. 440. Hauled. Dragged.
Harbinger, H. 414. Herald, Foreteller. St John i. 8.
Heresy, H. 215. Self-chosen error. Not the Church's teaching.
Homage, H. 142. The devotion of a man to his lord.

Implying, H. 64. Meaning 'Stephen' means 'a crown.'
Incarnate, H. 48. In the flesh. A man, 122, 138.
Ineffable, H. 167.⎫
Ineffably, H. 304.⎭ Not to be told in words, 178.

Laud, H. 98. Praise. 179, 227.
Legions, H. 305. Chosen troops.
Lenten, H. 90. The lengthening of the year. Spring. The forty days of fasting.
Litany, H. 463. A prayer of one in great distress.
Lore, H. 168. Learning. 411.

Mediator, H. 100. One who stands betwixt (amid) God and man.
Moil, H. 420. Drudgery. Dirt.
Mystic, H. 76, 86. Mysterious, 96, 129, 152, 168, 215. A God-taught truth.

Oblations, H. 76. Offerings. 413.
Orbs, H. 41. Worlds. The Stars.

Panoply, H. 270. Full Armour.

Paraclete, H. 385. The Comforter. The Holy Ghost.
Paschal, H. 90. Easter. 125, 127.
Passionless, H. 225. Without suffering.
Peer, H. 97. Equal.
Pent, H. 231. Shut up. Penned up.
Pentecostal, H. 152. Fiftieth day from Easter.
Phantoms, H. 15, 16. Ghosts.
Portals, H. 230. Gateways.
Potentate, H. 304. All-powerful over Time.
Predestinate, H. 40. To appoint.
Prevent, H. 33. Go before. Sing before daylight.
Primal, H. 14. First. Single.

Refection, H. 36. Refreshment. 226.
Retribution, H. 225. Reward. Recompense.
Retrieved, H. 61. Repaired. Brought back.
Rife, H. 39. Abundant. Full.
Rite, H. 309. An appointed ceremony.

Sages, H. 75. Wise men.
Sate, Satiate, } H. 105. Fill up full.
Schisms, H. 215. Divisions. Splits.
Seal, H. 29. Stamp, mark us as Thine.
Shrine, H. 345. Temple. Altar.
Supernal, H. 67. Supreme. Ruling above all.
Symbols, H. 385. Signs of.

Triune, H. 325. Three in One.
Trophy, H. 97. Sign of Victory, 304. Spoil, 300.
Type, H. 309. Impress. Mould of the antitype. The pattern
    set aside when the reality is present.

Unalloyed, H. 176. Without dross. Pure.
Unction, H. 157. Anointing. Soothing, 227.

Vanguard, H. 413. Front.
Vernal, H. 365. Spring. 387.
Vigil, H. 91. Watching. Being on guard, 124.
Vocation, H. 413. The call of the Holy Spirit.

Weal, H. 322. Well being. Good, 327.
Weltering, H. 418. Rolling.

Zealot, H. 406. Full of zeal, or Fermenting passion.

Any correction of Dates, Names and First Lines will be gratefully received by

R. M. COTTAGE,

N. Valence,

ALTON, Hants,

who being blind is not able to be as accurate as he wishes.

He puts out the pamphlet because he has not been able to find any cheap book like it for Choirs and Church persons who wish for information about the Hymns they sing;

And in the hope that it may suggest to the Clergy to give lectures on the Poets—Of the Eastern Church; Of the Early Western (St Ambrose); Of the later (St Gregory); Of the Middle Ages (St Bernard); Of the Reformation (Weiss and Sternhold); Of the 17th Century (Crossman and Ken); Of the Wesleyan movement; Of the Evangelical (Newton, Cowper); Of the High Church (Keble); Of the Catholic Reunion (Neale and Baker);—those many voices of the Church of God;

And on the Historic Continuity of "Ecclesia Anglicana." The Church of Bede, King Alfred, the Sarum Breviary, Magna Charta; Kethe, Mardley, Cosin, Tate, Heber and Wordsworth.

Readers should consult

The New Edition of Hymns A. and M. with Notes (preparing); The Rev. J. Ellerton's Notes on "Church Hymns," Notes on The Irish Church Hymnal; Prescott's Lectures, Biggs, Miller, Rogers, Christopher, Neale, Chandler, Winkworth, Kübler, Bunsen, Trench, Mone, Daniel.

CAMBRIDGE: PRINTED BY C. J. CLAY, M.A. & SON, AT THE UNIVERSITY PRESS.

www.ingramcontent.com/pod-product-compliance
Lightning Source LLC
Chambersburg PA
CBHW032123080426
42733CB00008B/1027